G.
CEN

CW00496350

Drama for Students, Volume 11

Staff

Editor: Elizabeth Thomason.

Contributing Editors: Anne Marie Hacht, Michael L. LaBlanc, Ira Mark Milne, Jennifer Smith.

Managing Editor: Dwayne Hayes.

Research: Victoria B. Cariappa, *Research Manager*. Cheryl Warnock, *Research Specialist*. Tamara Nott, Tracie A. Richardson, *Research Associates*. Nicodemus Ford, Sarah Genik, Timothy Lehnerer, *Research Assistants*.

Permissions: Maria Franklin, *Permissions Manager*. Sarah Tomasek, *Permissions Associate*.

Manufacturing: Mary Beth Trimper, *Manager, Composition and Electronic Prepress*. Evi Seoud, *Assistant Manager, Composition Purchasing and Electronic Prepress*. Stacy Melson, *Buyer*.

Imaging and Multimedia Content Team: Barbara

Yarrow, *Manager*. Randy Bassett, *Imaging Supervisor*. Robert Duncan, Dan Newell, *Imaging Specialists*. Pamela A. Reed, *Imaging Coordinator*. Leitha Etheridge-Sims, Mary Grimes, *Image Catalogers*. Robyn V. Young, *Project Manager*. Dean Dauphinais, *Senior Image Editor*. Kelly A. Quin, *Image Editor*.

Product Design Team: Kenn Zorn, *Product Design Manager*. Pamela A. E. Galbreath, *Senior Art Director*. Michael Logusz, *Graphic Artist*.

Copyright Notice

of this work have added value to the underlying factual material herein through one or more of the following: unique and original selection, coordination, expression, arrangement, and classification of the information. All rights to this publication will be vigorously defended.

Driving Miss Daisy

Alfred Uhry

1987

Introduction

Alfred Uhry had already been writing for musical theater for twenty-five years when his first nonmusical play *Driving Miss Daisy* became a surprise smash hit. Originally slated to run for five weeks at a small theater in New York City, demand for tickets was so high that it moved to a larger theater where it ran for about three years. Uhry also won the Pulitzer Prize in 1988. In his preface to the published play, Uhry commented on the experience.

> When I wrote this play I never dreamed I would be writing an introduction to it because I never thought it would get this far.... When I wonder how all this happened... I can come up with only one answer. I wrote what I knew to be the truth and people have recognized it as such.

Indeed, the numerous critics who lauded the play displayed remarkable similarity in their comments. They liked the play's sincerity, dignity, and honesty. Dealing with issues that plague all people—white or African American, northern or southern—the appeal of *Driving Miss Daisy* is universal.

Driving Miss Daisy went on to become an equally successful movie, winning best picture, best actress, and best screenplay adaptation for Uhry. Uhry's surprise success has also given him the freedom to continue pursuing his writing. In plays and musicals since *Driving Miss Daisy,* Uhry has continued to explore issues of concern to southern Jews, but his work is essentially about basic humanity.

Author Biography

Alfred Uhry was born around 1936 to an upper-middle-class German-Jewish family. He grew up in Atlanta, Georgia, where his father was a furniture designer. He left the South in 1958 to attend Brown University in Rhode Island, and he graduated with a degree in English. Uhry next moved to New York to begin his career in show business. He began collaborating with the composer Robert Waldman. Their play *The Robber Bridegroom*(1975) was their most successful, earning Uhry a Tony nomination and a Drama Desk nomination. It is a musical based on the southern writer Eudora Welty's novella. Uhry wrote the book and the lyrics. The play was a surprise hit Off-Broadway and moved to Broadway for the 1976-77 season.

He continued to work on other musicals, many of which closed on opening night or soon thereafter, or never even opened. To earn a living, he also wrote lyrics for television shows and commercials and also taught English and drama at a New York high school. In 1984, Uhry was struggling to get a workshop production of a musical about Al Capone off the ground and thinking about leaving theater. Suddenly, the idea came to him to write a play instead.

The characters in *Driving Miss Daisy*(1987) are based on people that Uhry knew growing up, including his grandmother and her African-

American chauffeur. The play, Uhry's first, was an instant success, quickly moving from the 74-seat Studio Theatre to another larger Off-Broadway theater and winning for Uhry another Drama Desk nomination. The play ran for three years. It was produced in regional theaters, by a national touring company, and in London, England. In 1988, it won a Pulitzer Prize.

It was also made into a movie. Uhry wrote the adaptation, for which he won an Academy Award. He had prior screenplay experience, having helped finish the script for the 1988 film *Mystic Pizza*. The film, *Driving Miss Daisy,* also won the 1990 Academy Award for best picture.

After his surprise hit, Uhry was approached by the Olympic Games Cultural Olympiad to produce a play for the 1996 Olympic Games that would be held in Atlanta. The play he wrote, *The Ghost of Ballyhoo,* won him another Tony Award the following year. In 1998, he wrote the book for the musical *Parade,* which played at Lincoln Center in New York.

Plot Summary

The play spans a period of twenty-five years in an unbroken series of segments. At the beginning of the play, Daisy Werthan, a seventy-two-year-old, southern Jewish widow, has just crashed her brand-new car while backing it out of the garage. After the accident, her son Boolie insists that she is not capable of driving. Over her protests, he hires a driver—Hoke Coleburn, an uneducated African American who is sixty. At first, Daisy wants nothing to do with Hoke. She is afraid of giving herself the airs of a rich person, even though Boolie is paying Hoke's salary. She strongly values her independence, so she also resents having someone around her house.

For the first week or so of Hoke's employment, Daisy refuses to let him drive her anywhere. He spends his time sitting in the kitchen. One day, however, he points out that a lady such as herself should not be taking the bus. He also points out that he is taking her son's money for doing nothing. Daisy responds by reminding Hoke that she does not come from a wealthy background, but she relents and allows him to drive her to the grocery store. She insists on maintaining control, however, telling him where to turn and how fast to drive. On another outing, she gets upset when he parks in front of the temple to pick her up, afraid that people will thinking she is giving herself airs.

One morning Boolie comes over after Daisy calls him up, extremely upset. She has discovered that Hoke is stealing from her—a can of salmon. She wants Boolie to fire Hoke right away. Her words also show her prejudice against African Americans. Boolie, at last, gives up. When Hoke arrives, Boolie calls him aside for a talk. First, however, Hoke wants to give something to Daisy— a can of salmon to replace the one he ate the day before. Daisy, trying to regain her dignity, says goodbye to Boolie.

Hoke continues to drive for Daisy. She also teaches him to read and write. When she gets a new car, he buys her old one from the dealer.

When Daisy is in her eighties, she makes a trip by car to Alabama for a family birthday party. She is upset that Boolie will not accompany her, but he and his wife are going to New York and already have theater tickets. On the trip, Daisy learns that this is Hoke's first time leaving Georgia. Suddenly, Daisy realizes that Hoke has taken a wrong turn. She gets frantic and wishes aloud that she had taken the train instead. The day is very long. It is after nightfall that they near Mobile. Hoke wants to stop to urinate, but Daisy forbids him from doing so as they are already late. At first Hoke obeys her, but then he pulls over to the side of the road. Daisy exclaims at his impertinence, but Hoke does not back down.

Hoke is exceedingly loyal to Daisy, but not so loyal that he does not use another job offer as leverage to get a pay raise. He tells Boolie how much he enjoys being fought over. One winter morning, there is an ice storm. The power has gone out and the roads are frozen over. On the telephone, Boolie tells Daisy he will be over as soon as the roads are clear. Right away, however, Hoke comes in. He has experience driving on icy roads from his days as a deliveryman. When Boolie calls back, Daisy tells him not to worry about coming over because Hoke is with her.

In the next segment, Daisy is on her way to temple, but there is a bad traffic jam. Hoke tells her that the temple has been bombed. Daisy is shocked and distressed. She says the temple is Reformed and can't understand why it was bombed. Hoke tells his own story of seeing his friend's father hanging from a tree, when he was just a boy. Daisy doesn't see why Hoke tells the story—it has nothing to do with the temple—and she doesn't even believe that Hoke got the truth. She refuses to see Hoke's linkage of prejudice against Jews and African Americans. Though she is quite upset by what has happened, she tries to deny it.

Another ten years or so has passed. Daisy and Boolie get into an argument about a Jewish organization's banquet for Martin Luther King, Jr. Daisy assumes Boolie will go with her, but he doesn't want to. He says it will hurt his business. Daisy plans on going, nonetheless. Hoke drives her to the dinner. At the last minute, she offhandedly invites Hoke to the dinner, but he refuses because she didn't ask him beforehand, like she would anyone else.

As Daisy gets older, she begins to lose her reason. One day Hoke must call Boolie because Daisy is having a delusion. She thinks she is a schoolteacher and she is upset because she can't find her students' papers. Before Boolie's arrival, she has a moment of clarity, and she tells Hoke that he is her best friend.

In the play's final segment, Daisy is ninetyseven and Hoke is eighty-five. Hoke no longer drives; instead, he relies on his granddaughter to get around. Boolie is about to sell Daisy's house—she has been living in a nursing home for two years. Hoke and Boolie go to visit her on Thanksgiving. She doesn't say much to either of them, but when Boolie starts talking she asks him to leave, reminding him that Hoke came to see her. She tries to pick up her fork and eat her pie. Hoke takes the plate and the fork from her and feeds her a small bite of pie.

Characters

Hoke Coleburn

Hoke is sixty years old when the play begins. He is an unemployed, uneducated African American. He has worked as a driver and delivery man previously. He is pleased when Boolie hires him, both for the job and because he likes to work for Jews. He is extremely patient with Daisy and tolerant of her barely disguised prejudices. He also is not afraid to speak up to her, always, however, in a quiet, respectful manner. When his dignity is at stake, he speaks up for his rights. His integrity teaches Daisy how to be a more humane person. Hoke also develops as a result of their friendship, for instance, Daisy teaches him to read. Perhaps most importantly, the financial security Hoke obtains over the twenty-five years brings him greater self-confidence and self-respect.

Media Adaptations

- Uhry wrote the screenplay adaptation for 1989's *Driving Miss Daisy*. The movie starred Jessica Tandy, Morgan Freeman, and Dan Ackroyd. Bruce Beresford directed it. Warner Home Video released it in 1990.

Daisy

Daisy is a seventy-two-year-old widow living alone when the play opens. She is independent and stubborn, but her son Boolie insists on hiring a driver for her after she crashes her car while backing out of the garage. Daisy deeply resents Hoke and the implication that she is no longer able to control her own life. However, Hoke's mild manner eventually wins her over, and she finally allows him to drive her to the market. He serves as her driver for the next twenty-five years. Through her friendship with Hoke, Daisy loses some of her deep-rooted prejudice against African Americans and even comes to consider herself a supporter of civil rights. Although she becomes unable to care for herself as she gets older, eventually moving to a nursing home, she never loses her determination or her sense of self. Some of the characteristics that identified her at the beginning of the play, such as her bossiness or her sense of humor, are with her as strongly at the end of the play.

Boolie Werthan

Boolie is Daisy's son. He is forty years old when the play begins. He has taken over his father's printing company, and, over the course of the play, he develops into one of the city's leading business figures. As the years pass, he becomes more conscious of how he will be perceived by society, and, consequently, does not want to attend the United Jewish Appeal banquet for Martin Luther King, Jr. Boolie takes good care of his mother, but he sometimes neglects her feelings. When her opinion disagrees with his, he generally overrides her without thinking about what she really wants or why she wants it. However, he humors his mother's stubbornness rather than try to understand it.

Florine Werthan

Although Boolie's wife Florine is never seen by the audience, she is still a lively character. She is Jewish but socializes with the Christian community and surrounds herself with Christian trappings, such as Christmas decorations. She has high social aspirations and is a member of many organizations. She values social status and symbols more than she does family, and primarily because of this, Daisy thinks she is shallow and foolish.

Race and Prejudice

Race and prejudice are important themes in the play. Prejudice is demonstrated against both African Americans and Jews. Several brief statements remind readers of the situation for African Americans in the South. Hoke tells Boolie that he has had a hard time finding a job, for "[T]hey hirin' young if they hirin' colored." Years later, Hoke refers to the fact that African Americans cannot use white facilities. Prejudice against Jews is demonstrated through the bombing of the temple and Boolie's reference to businessmen who dislike and stereotype Jews. He recognizes their belief that "as long as you got to deal with Jews, the really smart ones come from New York." Hoke also specifically mentions the way many Southerners feel toward Jews: "People always talkin' 'bout they stingy and they cheap, but doan' say none of that roun' me."

Daisy, herself a Jew, feels prejudice against African Americans, though she denies it. When the play opens, Daisy refers to African Americans as "them," which does not escape Boolie's notice. After she is convinced that Hoke is stealing from her, she becomes more aggressive in her accusations. "They all take things, you know," she tells Boolie. Later in the same scene, she even says,

"They are like having little children in the house. They want something so they just take it. Not a smidgin of manners. No conscience." She also mimics the speech of uneducated African Americans like Hoke: "'Nome,' he'll say." Daisy's accusations, which indict all African Americans, backfire when Hoke brings her a new can of salmon. She can no longer hold his actions against an entire race. Throughout the course of the play, however, Daisy begins to lose her prejudices. She even argues with Boolie about their presence at a banquet honoring civil rights leader Martin Luther King, Jr.

Despite this change, she still does not see the prejudiced world around her clearly, and does not understand that some white Southerners dislike Jews as much as they dislike African Americans. When the temple is bombed, she is certain it must be a mistake—"I'm sure they meant to bomb one of the conservative synagogues or the orthodox one. The temple is reform"—or that Hoke misheard the police officer. Hoke, however, understands better than Daisy. "It doan' matter to them people," he says. "A Jew is a Jew to them folks. Jes' like light or dark we all the same nigger." Daisy refuses to believe this, for even though she makes great strides in combating her prejudice, she still feels superior to Hoke, for many reasons: she is wealthier, she is his employer, and she is white. Because of this innate feeling, she does not invite Hoke to attend the King banquet with her until virtually the last minute. Hoke pridefully refuses, knowing that it is only because she takes him for granted that she did not speak with him about it sooner.

Friendship

The relationship between Daisy and Hoke is at the heart of this play. When Daisy first meets Hoke, she dislikes him, both because he is African American and because she resents his presence in her home. Over the years, she comes to grow fond of Hoke, though her gruff speech would not indicate this. Both Hoke and Daisy, however, understand the feelings that they share. On the day of the ice storm, Hoke drives to her home despite the slick roads. He wants to be there for Daisy, whom he knows will be alone. Although Daisy is "*[T]JouchecT*" and calls his actions "sweet," she still reproves him for tracking dirt into her kitchen. Hoke says, "Now Miz Daisy, what you think I am? A mess?" Though Daisy responds in the affirmative, the stage directions note, *"This is an old routine between them and not without affection."* It is not until Daisy is much older—and getting occasionally confused—that she puts her feelings into words. "You're my best friend," she tells Hoke, and she takes hold of his hand. It seems likely that she wants to express her feelings for Hoke while she is still able to do so.

Topics for Further Study

- One way that actors "get into" their roles is to imagine their characters in situations that are implied but not included in the play. Try to imagine these characters in other situations and write another short scene for inclusion in the play.

- Imagine that Hoke overheard the conversation between Boolie and Daisy in which she implies that all African Americans are dishonest. How do you think he would react to such statements?

- Conduct research to find out more about how racial relations have changed in the South from the 1940s to the present day. Write a paragraph about your findings.

- Imagine that you are from another country and know nothing about race relations in the twentieth-century South. What might be your impression of race relations based solely on *Driving Miss Daisy*?

- Read another play that portrays a Southern point of view and Southern issues. Tennessee Williams' *A Streetcar Named Desire* would be a good choice. How does the image of the South differ in the two plays? How is at alike?

- Toward the end of the play, Daisy exclaims to Boolie, "I've never been prejudiced and you know it!" How do you think Hoke would respond? How would you respond?

Growing Old

An important theme in the play is growing old. The play spans twenty-five years. By its end, Daisy is ninety-seven, Hoke is eighty-five, and Boolie is sixty-five. The characters all experience changes over the years. Daisy becomes more liberal, while Boolie becomes more conservative. Daisy and Hoke also become good friends. The two share the knowledge of the difficulties of aging. When Daisy grows confused, thinking that she is still a teacher, she says to Hoke, "I'm being trouble. Oh God, I don't want to be trouble to anybody." She realizes that her aging is making her more difficult, and she is afraid that she will become a burden. Hoke points out that she at least has the benefit of aging in comfort. "You want something to cry about, I take you to the state home, show you what layin' out dere in de halls."

Eventually, Boolie puts Daisy in a nursing home. The stage directions note that "*[S]he seems fragile and diminished, but still vital.*" Her aging has not made her unwilling to speak her mind. "Go charm the nurses," she tells Boolie when she wants him to leave. Though she is unable to feed herself very well, she still has her mind.

For his part, Hoke has changed too. He can no longer drive and, instead, must rely on his granddaughter to chauffeur him around. Through Hoke's inability to drive, the play also demonstrates that as people get older, they lose their independence, in a sense, becoming more like children again. Hoke is unable to visit Daisy often because the bus doesn't go to the nursing home. Hoke admits that "it hard [to visit Daisy], not drivin'." At this point in their lives, people like Daisy and Hoke must rely on others for almost everything—even for the maintenance of cherished friendships.

Symbolism

Daisy's automobiles (of which there are many) are central symbols in the play. For Daisy, driving her own car represents freedom. This freedom is taken away from her when Boolie hires Hoke. For Hoke, Daisy's cars—the Oldsmobile that he purchases used from the dealer after Boolie gets Daisy a new car—represents a rise in social status. "Keep them ashes off my 'polstry," he warns Boolie, as the two men drive to the dealership. For Boolie, however, the car is just an object, a large, dangerous object in the hands of his mother, which he places in the hands of a driver he can trust.

Even when Daisy relents and allows Hoke to drive her car—in a sense, take away her freedom—she does her best to continue to assert herself. On their first trip together, Daisy tries to instruct Hoke on the route to take. "I want to go to it [the Piggly Wiggly] the way I always go," she says, demonstrating her fixation with being in charge of herself. Hoke, however, rejects her orders, refusing to turn as she tells him to, because he knows a better route to the store. This exchange shows each person's basic nature: Daisy's stubborn insistence on denying that change can occur, and Hoke's quiet yet resolute manner of teaching Daisy to accept change.

Daisy's house also has symbolic meaning. Like the car, it symbolizes her independence. She feels she should be in charge of her house, thus when Boolie hires Hoke, her control of this sphere is undermined. The other characters recognize what the house means to Daisy. Boolie does not sell it until she has been in the nursing home for several years and will never come home. "It feels funny to sell the house while Mama's still alive," he says to Hoke, "I know I'm doing the right thing." He looks to Hoke for affirmation, which he finds, but he also admits that he is not going to tell his mother what he is doing. Hoke also agrees with this decision. Both men know that Daisy will not idly abide the only symbol of her independent adulthood being taken away.

Setting

Almost the entire play takes place in Atlanta, Georgia. Daisy has spent her life in the city, though she grew up in a much poorer section of town. She is a part of Atlanta's Jewish community. She belongs to a temple and takes part in Jewish cultural events. Boolie has also spent his life in Atlanta. He has taken over his father's printing business, and he becomes a leading figure in the city's circle of businessmen. Though his wife, Florine, is also Jewish, she socializes within the Christian community because it gives her higher status.

Even though Atlanta is a thriving city, the atmosphere is more that of a small town. The people within Daisy's social circle are all well acquainted. Even Hoke has a connection to the Werthans prior to working as Daisy's chauffeur. He used to work for a Jewish judge whom Boolie knows.

Although Daisy leads an insular life, she does get out of the city. Boolie, as well, takes trips to New York. Hoke, however, has never left Georgia before he drives Daisy to attend a funeral in Alabama. Hoke originally comes from a farm near Macon, and his recollection of the lynching of his friend's father serves as a reminder of the racial violence that regularly took place in the rural South. Although his family also lives in Atlanta, they clearly belong to the generations of African Americans who leave the South, or if staying there, make the choice to do so. His daughter, married to a train porter, has visited northern cities such as New York and Detroit and urges her father to do so. His granddaughter still lives in Atlanta, but she is an educated scientist, teaching at an African-American college.

Structure

The play has no specific acts and scenes. Instead, it is divided up into segments, some of which flow one into the other, others that do not. The play also spans twenty-five years, so sometimes large amounts of time pass between segments. This structure frees the action of the play from time or plot constraints. Uhry can create exactly which incidents he believes will be the most evocative.

The structure also emphasizes the compactness of the characters' lives. Though the fluid structure would seem to indicate that little changes over the course of twenty-five years, that is not the play's reality.

The 1940s

After the end of World War II, American society and economy saw significant changes. During the war, many women, Mexican Americans, and African Americans were employed in defense factories. After the war ended, however, as government measures encouraged employers to hire veterans, many of these people lost their jobs. Congress even abolished the Fair Employment Practices Committee, which had protected African Americans from job discrimination. Overall, however, unemployment remained low, and incomes increased. Even though the economy experienced dramatic inflation, many Americans, who had scrimped during the war years, were eager to spend their savings. Rising consumerism helped lead to a new era of prosperity.

Compare & Contrast

- **1950s:** Of a total U.S. population of close to 164.3 million in 1955, around 7.4 million are aged between 65 and 79, or 4.5 percent.

  1990s: Of a total U.S. population of 273.9 million in 1998, just over 18 million are aged between 65 and 79, or 6.6 percent.

- **1950s:** In 1956, the Supreme Court rules that segregated transportation systems are illegal.

  1960s: In 1960, the Supreme Court rules that segregation in certain public facilities is illegal.

  1970s: In 1971, the Supreme Court upholds affirmative actions programs in schools and businesses.

  1990s: In 1996, the Supreme Court hears a case involving allegations that federal prosecutors in Los Angeles selectively pursued and charged blacks in crack cocaine cases. The Court finds that the African-American defendants are unable to prove the allegations, so the guilty charge stands.

- **1950s and 1960s:** African Americans stage numerous boycotts, marches, and sit-ins to protest segregation laws in the South.

  1990s: Since passage of the Civil Rights Act of 1964, discrimination in employment and in public accommodations has been illegal.

- **Mid-1960s:** In 1964, less than 6 percent of eligible African Americans in Mississippi are registered to vote.

Late 1960s: By 1968, 59 percent of African Americans in Mississippi are registered to vote.

1990s: In 1990, 31.5 percent of African Americans of voting age in Mississippi are registered to vote.

- **1960s:** In 1969, only about 1,500 African Americans hold elected office.

1970s: By the end of the decade, more than 4,500 African Americans hold elected office.

1990s: In 1997, there are 8,617 elected African-American officials throughout the United States.

- **1960s:** In 1964, only about 200,000 African Americans attend college.

1970s: By the end of the decade, more than 800,000 African Americans attend college.

1990s: In 1994, about 36.7 percent of African Americans, out of a total population of 32.5 million, attended two-or four-year colleges.

President Harry S. Truman ran for reelection in 1948. His stand on civil rights became an important issue in the campaign. Two years earlier, in 1946, African-American civil rights groups had urged Truman to act against racism. African Americans faced segregation and discrimination in housing and employment. African Americans in many areas continued to be lynched, a crime that the courts ignored. Also, Southern African Americans were prevented from voting through the use of poll taxes.

In 1948, Truman banned racial discrimination in the military and in federal jobs. In response, Southern Democrats formed their own party, one that called for continued racial segregation. Despite these party divisions, Truman won the presidency.

The Civil Rights Movement

African Americans began taking a more active stance in the 1950s to end discrimination in the United States. During the 1950s, the Supreme Court ordered the desegregation of schools and transportation systems. President Dwight Eisenhower signed the Civil Rights Act of 1957. The first civil right law passed since Reconstruction, this act made it a federal crime to prevent any qualified person from voting. The Reverend Martin Luther King, Jr., also emerged as an important civil rights leader. He urged the use of nonviolent resistance to bring about the end of racial discrimination. King was assassinated in 1968.

In the 1960s, civil rights activists continued to challenge racist policies in interstate transportation and voter registration. The Civil Rights Act of 1964 was passed, barring discrimination in employment and public accommodations, and giving the Justice Department the power to enforce school desegregation. Congress also passed the Voting Rights Act of 1965, which put the voter registration process under federal control. Within three years, over half of all eligible African Americans in the South had registered to vote.

Despite these successes, many African Americans grew to question the effectiveness of nonviolent protest. Some felt they should use violence for self-defense, while others did not want to integrate into white society at all. These African Americans adopted the slogan "Black Power," which became widely used by the late 1960s. They wanted greater economic and political power and even complete separation from white society.

Throughout the 1970s, African Americans, as well as other minority groups, continued to fight for equal rights. President Richard Nixon, however, vowed to not ask for any new civil rights legislation. When the Supreme Court ruled in 1971 that busing could be used to integrate schools, he denounced their decision. By the middle of the decade, more African Americans were enrolling in college, holding professional jobs, and serving in public office. African-American political leaders formed strong alliances and effective lobbies.

Women and Society

Although popular culture in the 1950s presented the ideal woman as a full-time suburban homemaker, many women in that decade held jobs outside the home. By the 1960s, the women's movement was experiencing a widespread revival. Betty Friedan's 1963 book *The Feminine Mystique* vehemently rejected the popular notion that women were content with fulfilling the roles of wife, mother, and homemaker. Friedan charged that many women felt stifled by this domestic life. The National Organization for Women, a women's rights group, was formed in 1966, and more and more women joined the movement throughout the 1970s.

The National Women's Political Caucus, founded in 1971, encouraged women to run for political office. Women's leaders believed that women in public office would contribute to the shaping of public policy in favor of equal rights. In 1972, Congress passed the Education Amendments Act, which outlawed sexual discrimination in higher education. Many all-male schools began to allow women to enroll. The women's rights movement, however, failed to win passage of the Equal Rights Amendment, or ERA, a constitutional amendment barring discrimination on the basis of sex. Although Congress passed the ERA in 1972, not enough states ratified the bill, therefore it never became a law.

The Aging Population

Several measures contributed to a changing lifestyle for elderly Americans. President Lyndon B. Johnson initiated the Medicare program in 1965, which offered national health insurance to people over the age of 65. Americans were living longer, so by the 1970s, the aging population contributed to a dramatic rise in U.S. spending on health care—from $74 billion in 1970 to around $884 billion in 1993.

Driving Miss Daisy was the first play that Alfred Uhry wrote and he based it on people he had known growing up in the South, particularly his grandmother and her driver. The play's original schedule called for it to run for five weeks at Playwrights Horizon, a New York nonprofit theater that seated an audience of seventy-four. When the five-week run was up, the play was extended another five weeks, and when that was up, the play moved to a bigger theater. A year and a half later, the show was still playing in New York, and also around the country. Uhry also won the Pulitzer Prize.

Audiences and critics immediately responded to the play, even when its premise seemed distinctly unpromising. In *American Theatre,* Don Shewey recalls his experience.

> I remember trudging upstairs... to see a play that sounded distinctly unpromising. It was about—gads!— an elderly white woman and her black chauffeur. On one hand, it sounded politically unsavory: Have we progressed no further than portraying African-Americans onstage as servants. On the other hand, it sounded theatrically too dreary for words: How could it be

anything but a parade of predictable Sunday-school pieties about how we're all alike under the skin and we should all get along? I personally resisted every inch of the way the feeling I left the theatre with that night: Wow, [this] is a good play!

Critics commented on the play's appeal, in fact, often using that very word. In the *New York Times,* Mel Gussow refers to the play's "homespun appeal" and its "renewed sincerity." Robert Brustein writes in the *New Republic* that the play "has both appealing brevity and considerable quality." He calls viewing the play "an experience of considerable power and sensitivity." These critics, along with others, responded to the play's basic humanity and the truths it told. "It is the work of decent people," writes Brustein, "working against odds to show how humans still manage to reach out to each other in a divided world." Judy Lee Oliva, in *Contemporary Dramatists,* says that *"Driving Miss Daisy* is a play about dignity in which all the characters strive to hold onto their personal integrity."

The play deftly presents an overview of the changing values and times in the South. Spanning from 1948 to 1972, the play alludes to important themes of the twentieth century, such as racism and prejudice. Its focus on the relationship between two people allows for a more personalized view of historical realities. Oliva notes that the play is "representative of a time in history and tells about that time via this one story." However, as Gussow points out, "history remains background. The principal story is the personal relationship, the interdependence of the two irrevocably allied Southerners."

Critics overwhelmingly warmed to the characters, who carried this play smoothly along: the crusty Daisy and the restrained but prideful Hoke. Gussow declares that the play sometimes "seems more like an extended character sketch or family memoir than an actual drama." Even Florine, the invisible character, emerges, "deftly characterized by the playwright," writes Brustein, "with simple strokes through Daisy's attitude toward her."

Uhry's subtlety of writing was also appreciated. Oliva calls Uhry "a master of understatement." Notes Gussow, "The play remains quiet, and it becomes disarming, as it delineates the characters with almost offhand glimpses." He uses Hoke's casual declaration "The first time I left Georgia was 25 minutes ago" as an example of this technique. Oliva further believes that *Driving Miss Daisy* was distinguished from other plays of the decade by "the subtlety with which the playwright empowers his dramaturgy, enabling him to address issues of race and ethnicity and to explore conflicts of old versus young, rich versus poor, Jew versus gentile, while maintaining the emphasis on the very human relationship that develops between Daisy and Hoke."

Even after its New York run ended, *Driving*

Miss Daisy remained with the American audience. Uhry adapted it into a film that came out in 1989. Like the play, it garnered numerous positive reviews including one from Vincent Canby of the *New York Times* who declared it to be "the most successful stage-to-screen translation" since *Dangerous Liaisons. Driving Miss Daisy* went on to win Academy Awards for best actress, best screenplay adaptation, and best film.

What Do I Read Next?

- Uhry's second play, *The Last Night of Ballyhoo*(1997) tackles the unexplored aspects of southern anti-Semitism. Uhry again returns to the affluent Jewish community in Atlanta.

- Carson McCuller's novel *The Heart is a Lonely Hunter*(1940) draws on the Southern gothic tradition of

American literature. The novel's protagonists—including a man who is deaf and mute, an African-American doctor, and a widower—all live in a Georgia mill town and are drawn together by their outsider status.

- Lorraine Hansberry's three-act play *A Raisin in the Sun*(1959) explores what happens in 1940s Chicago when an African-American family attempts to move into an all-white neighborhood. This drama reflects Hansberry's own experiences of racial harassment.

- Evan O'Connell's novel *Mrs. Bridge* (1959) chronicles the adult life of Mrs. Bridge, a well-off Midwestern matron. Though she enjoys life's comforts, Mrs. Bridge feels isolated from her husband and her three children.

- Uhry's first theatrical success was based on the musical adaptation of Eudora Welty's novel *The Robber Bridegroom*(1942). This fairy tale tells the story of a highwayman who masquerades part-time as a gentleman. He kidnaps a planter's daughter, and she falls in love with him. The novel contains gothic horror, mystery, and magic.

- *Fried Green Tomatoes at the Whistle Stop Cafe*(1987) by Fannie Flagg tells the extraordinary friendship of two Southern women. After helping her friend escape from an abusive marriage, Idgie and Ruth set up a small cafe where everyone was welcome. The story is told through reminiscences of aging characters as well as in the small-town past.

Sources

Brustein, Robert, Review of *Driving Miss Daisy* in *New Republic,* Vol. 197, No. 13, September 28, 1987, pp. 28-30.

Canby, Vincent, "'Miss Daisy,' Chamber Piece from the Stage" in *New York Times,* December 13, 1989, p. C19.

Gussow, Mel, Review of *Driving Miss Daisy* in *New York Times,* April 16, 1987, p. C22.

Oliva, Judy Lee, "Alfred Uhry: Overview," in *Contemporary Dramatists,* 5th ed., edited by K. A. Berney, St. James Press, 1993.

Shewey, Don, "Ballyhoo and Daisy, Too" in *American Theatre,* Vol. 14, April, 1997, p. 24-27.

Uhry, Alfred, Preface to *Driving Miss Daisy,* Theatre Communications Group, 1986.

Further Reading

Shewey, Don, "Ballyhoo and Daisy, Too," in *American Theatre,* April, 1997, p. 24-27.

> This article surrounds a talk between Shewey and Uhry about several of his plays, providing a unique look at Uhry's perspective of his work.

Sterritt, David, "A Voice for Themes Other Entertainers Have Left Behind," in *Christian Science Monitor,* July 29, 1997, p. 15.

> This article discusses Uhry's work in relation to prevailing attitudes toward morality in the United States.

Lightning Source UK Ltd.
Milton Keynes UK
UKHW041120121219
355254UK00012B/1184/P